Who Was
Napoleon?

by Jim Gigliotti

illustrated by Gregory Copeland

Penguin Workshop
An Imprint of Penguin Random House

For Carmela, because the hand that rocks the cradle
rules the world—JG

To the "Box"—GC

PENGUIN WORKSHOP
Penguin Young Readers Group
An Imprint of Penguin Random House LLC

Text copyright © 2018 by Jim Gigliotti. Illustrations copyright © 2018 by
Penguin Random House LLC. All rights reserved. Published by Penguin Workshop,
an imprint of Penguin Random House LLC, 345 Hudson Street, New York,
New York 10014. PENGUIN and PENGUIN WORKSHOP are trademarks of
Penguin Books Ltd. WHO HQ & Design is a registered trademark of
Penguin Random House LLC. Printed in the USA.

Library of Congress Cataloging-in-Publication Data is available.

ISBN 9780448488608 (paperback)   10 9 8 7 6 5 4 3 2 1
ISBN 9781524788537 (library binding)   10 9 8 7 6 5 4 3 2 1

Contents

Who Was Napoleon?

One day early in 1784, a heavy snowstorm covered the grounds of the military school for boys in Brienne, France. There was so much snow that the students couldn't get their usual exercise after class. But fourteen-year-old Napoleon Bonaparte had an idea: snowball fight!

This being a military school, however, Napoleon wasn't thinking about any ordinary snowball fight. Instead, he wanted the boys to put to use what they had been learning in the classroom. They built forts and dug trenches. On

Napoleon's orders, a snowball war began. It lasted two full weeks during the times that the boys weren't in class. Some days, Napoleon commanded one side. Some days, he commanded the other.

The snowball war wasn't entirely harmless. After a while, small rocks got mixed in with the hard ice. Those snowballs hurt! So the school put an end to it. Napoleon's first "war" was over.

The teachers weren't happy about their students getting hurt. But they *were* happy to see Napoleon take charge. Ever since he arrived at the school four years earlier, he had been moody and quiet. He didn't have a lot of friends. But he seemed happy to lead the school's snowball battles.

Little did his teachers know that Napoleon would go on to become one of the most famous military commanders in the history of the world. He would lead hundreds of thousands of men into battle. And with a combination of courage and strategy, he won most of the battles he fought.

Napoleon went on to build a vast empire for France. At the height of his career, he ruled over more than seventy million people. To the French people,  Napoleon was a good guy. To his enemies, he was not. Late in Napoleon's life, those same enemies defeated him and sent him to live on a tiny island. There, he had plenty of time to talk about his memories.

"What a novel my life has been!" Napoleon exclaimed one day to the assistant who was writing it all down.

Napoleon's life had it all: friends and enemies, politics and war, a love story, and so much more. And Napoleon himself—the main character—was famous, clever, and brave. But a novel is a made-up story. Napoleon lived it all for real.

CHAPTER 1
Island Beginnings

Napoleon Bonaparte's life began in Corsica, a small island in the Mediterranean Sea. Corsica is about fifty miles west of what is now Italy and one hundred miles southeast of France.

For almost five hundred years, Corsica had belonged to Genoa, a city that is now part of Italy. But the Corsican people wanted to be free. They often fought with soldiers from Genoa. When the government of Genoa grew tired of the fighting, they sold the island to the French in 1768.

That upset the Corsicans even more! They didn't believe they should be bought and sold. And so they started fighting the French. But at that time France was one of the most powerful nations in the world. It easily conquered the island.

When Napoleon was born in Ajaccio, Corsica, on August 15, 1769, he automatically became a French citizen. But the influence of hundreds of years of Italian rule on Corsica didn't go away overnight: Napoleon, like most of the people on Corsica, spoke Italian.

Napoleon's father was named Carlo and his mother was named Letizia. Even though they

helped Corsica fight the French before Napoleon's birth, his parents knew there was no use keeping up the fight after the battle was lost. They grew to respect the new French government. Napoleon's father even changed his first name from Carlo to Charles because it sounded less Italian. He changed the family's last name from Buonaparte to Bonaparte because it sounded more French.

Life was not easy on the island. Most of the people in Ajaccio were craftsmen or fishermen. Charles was a lawyer, and Napoleon's family had more money than many in the town, but no one there was very rich.

The Bonapartes lived in a nice house and had a couple of servants. They grew much of their food on their land. Their four-story home even had a mill downstairs that was used to grind flour for making bread. They had a

vineyard to make wine and an olive grove to make olive oil. But the family had money to spend only on the basics: clothing for their children and any food that couldn't be grown on their land.

And there were many children to clothe and mouths to feed! Napoleon had four brothers and three sisters. Napoleon was the second-oldest child. His older brother Joseph had been born in 1768. His other brothers were Lucien, Louis, and Jerome. Napoleon's sisters were Elisa, Pauline, and Caroline.

Napoleon was the most willful of the large group. He had a terrible temper, and he didn't always tell the truth. His family called him a troublemaker. Napoleon never was in serious

trouble, though. Once in a while, he was punished for fighting, but even that didn't seem to be a big deal. After all, the grown-ups on Corsica had been fighting battles all their lives. Napoleon fit right in.

Napoleon practiced fighting with a wooden sword. He and his friends in Ajaccio would pretend to be soldiers. They set up battles that lasted all day long. Napoleon was always in charge of his side. When it was too dark to play outside anymore, they picked up the next day where they had left off. Some of the play battles lasted for days at a time. Days turned into weeks, and weeks into months. Napoleon loved playing war!

When Napoleon was about five years old, he began going to school. Every day, his mother sent him off with some white bread for lunch. And every day on the way to school, he traded his bread to a French soldier for one of his daily rations.

The white bread was soft and fresh. The soldier's brown bread was hard and old. But, Napoleon explained to his mother, "If I am going to be a soldier, I must get used to eating soldiers' bread."

In school, Napoleon was good at geography, and he was very good at math. Mostly, though, he loved reading about history. He wanted to know all he could about famous battles and military heroes, such as Alexander the Great. He dreamed of one day becoming a conquering hero just like Alexander.

Alexander the Great (356–323 BC)

Alexander III, who came to be called Alexander the Great, is sometimes considered the greatest military commander in history. He was king of Macedonia (what is today northern and central Greece) from 336 to 323 BC. Through military conquests, he built a huge empire that stretched from Greece to India. He ruled over territory covering some two million square miles. Alexander never lost a battle, even when he was greatly outnumbered by his opponents.

CHAPTER 2
Birth of a Military Career

In 1777, Charles Bonaparte sailed to France. Because of his family history and his position as a lawyer in Corsica, he had become an important person in the island government. The leader of Corsica sent Charles to France to represent his country in the government there.

Charles turned out to be good at politics, though he often worked for his personal gain. He once obtained government funding for a grove of mulberry trees he later made a profit on. More importantly for Napoleon, Charles was able to arrange for scholarships to military school for his two oldest sons.

One of the requirements for the scholarships was that the boys had to speak French. And so, in December 1778, nine-year-old Napoleon and his brother Joseph sailed to the French town of Autun. They spent several months at school there, learning the language. Joseph stayed to

study for the priesthood in the Roman Catholic religion. Napoleon moved on to a military school in Brienne.

Napoleon spent five years in Brienne. He learned how to build a fort, which came in handy for the snowball fights, but much of his schoolwork was traditional. He took classes in math, Latin, history, geography, and music. He was the best in his class at math. Napoleon sometimes helped his fellow students with their math in exchange for their help in subjects he wasn't as good at, such as Latin.

But Napoleon didn't feel as if he fit in at Brienne. Many of the other kids picked on him. In part, it was because they considered him a foreigner. Even though he had learned to speak French, it was with a heavy Corsican accent. They made fun of the way he talked, and they bragged that the French had conquered his island. Mostly, though, it was because they came from wealthy and influential families in France—and Napoleon did not.

Social status was very important in French society. Rich people (the upper classes) didn't often associate with poor people (the lower classes). And people with less money could not compete for the best jobs or obtain the same rank in the military as people from wealthy families. Napoleon felt like an outsider—and he was treated like one.

The Class System in France

At the time of Napoleon's birth, France was a monarchy and was ruled by a king. After the king and queen, who ranked above all, French society was divided into three classes called estates. The First Estate was the Roman Catholic clergy, including bishops and cardinals. The Second Estate consisted of wealthy noble families. And the Third Estate included everyone else: peasants, shopkeepers, farmers, and more.

Although the Third Estate was by far the largest group, the First and Second Estates had more influence with the king.

FRANCE
Pre - 1789

1st Estate
Clergy

2nd Estate
Nobility

3rd Estate
Everyone
Else

Napoleon didn't like the class system in France. The attitudes of the other students at Brienne upset Napoleon. He didn't think their luxurious lifestyles could ever prepare them for being soldiers. Because Napoleon didn't have many friends at school, he kept to himself much of the time. He spent many hours reading in the school library and working hard at his studies.

Napoleon worked so hard that in October 1784, he was selected to be part of a small group of five students who left Brienne. They were chosen to continue their military studies at the École Militaire (say: AY-cole mee-lee-TAIR) in the famous city of Paris, France. This was a great honor!

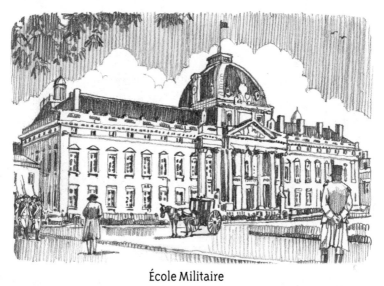

École Militaire

At the École Militaire, Napoleon felt like he really was in the army. He woke up each morning to the sound of a bugler. He wore a fancy uniform.

He learned to march in formation, load a cannon, and read a map.

Napoleon was only fifteen when his father died, in February 1785, from stomach cancer. Eight months later, Napoleon graduated from the École Militaire. It took him just over one year to complete studies that took most of the students two years! But his hard work had paid off:

When Napoleon joined the French army in the city of Valence, he began his army career as an officer. His officer's salary helped him support his entire family back in Corsica.

CHAPTER 3
Changing Times

Napoleon entered the army in November 1785 as an artillery lieutenant. (*Artillery* is the term for large guns. At the time, an army's large guns were cannons.) Captain was the next step up the ladder. In those days, that was about as far as someone with Napoleon's upbringing could go.

It didn't matter how good a soldier was at his job. The higher positions were given to people from upper-class families.

But things were changing fast in France. The French Revolution, which began in 1789, helped make it possible to earn a promotion by doing a good job. Napoleon had been in the military fewer than four years when the French Revolution started.

Poor harvests and heavy taxes left many French peasants begging for food. They were frustrated

and hungry, while members of the First and Second Estates lived in palaces and had plenty of food to eat. So the Third Estate began fighting for a more equal society. Their famous motto was *"Liberté, égalité, fraternité."* Those are the French words for *liberty* (freedom), *equality* (fairness), and *fraternity* (brotherhood).

Napoleon didn't pick sides in the early days of the French Revolution. He never did like the

class system, but he was determined to stay out of the fight. He didn't want his career ruined by choosing the wrong side. He left the army and sailed back to Corsica. There, he organized the Corsican National Guard and began writing a history of the island. But the royalist leader of Corsica and Napoleon did not get along. Eventually, Napoleon and his family were sent away from their island home—for good.

The French Revolution

The French Revolution began on July 14, 1789. That was the day a mob of citizens attacked a prison called the Bastille and freed the prisoners there.

Over the next several years, the revolutionaries fiercely fought against wealthy citizens who were loyal to the king. The revolutionaries were called republicans. The king's supporters were called royalists. There were far more republicans than

royalists, and the republicans won. They formed
their own government and arrested King Louis XVI
and his wife, Queen Marie-Antoinette. Louis XVI and
Marie-Antoinette were both charged with treason
and put to death in 1793.

In June 1793, Napoleon sailed with his mother, three brothers, and three sisters to France. (Joseph was already there.) He would never again return to Corsica. He rejoined the French army. He was defending the new republican government, which had taken power away from the king. They wanted an assembly of representatives elected by the people.

While the French Revolution brought an end to King Louis XVI's reign, the trouble didn't end there. The royalists continued to fight to bring back the monarchy. The wealthy nobles had always benefited from having a king rather than elected officials. And that led to Napoleon's first big moment on the battlefield.

Late in 1793, the royalists got help from some pretty powerful friends who wanted them to regain power. Countries such as Great Britain, Spain, and the Dutch Republic saw what happened when people fought for change in France. They knew if it happened there, it could happen in their countries, too. So they joined together and soon were at war with France.

They wanted to bring back the monarchy. And in 1793, the British navy helped the royalists take over the city of Toulon in southern France. Toulon was important because its harbor was a base for French ships.

Napoleon was not far away from Toulon on an assignment for the army. When the officer in charge of the artillery at Toulon was injured in the fighting, the republicans sent for Napoleon.

Some of the French leaders thought the situation in Toulon was hopeless. They didn't think the city could be taken back from the powerful British navy. But Napoleon had incredible confidence in his abilities. "You tell me it is impossible," he liked to say. "There is no such word in French."

At Toulon, Napoleon sent his men into the countryside, where many republicans lived. He told them to get whatever horses, men, and supplies they could find. When they came back, he attacked the fort the French royalists held.

During the fighting, Napoleon was wounded in his thigh by an enemy's bayonet—a blade attached to the end of a long gun. Blood poured from the wound. But Napoleon wasn't about to be stopped. He kept fighting until the republicans captured the fort. Then he turned his cannons on the British ships in the harbor. The cannonballs were too much for them. They left the harbor and headed back to Britain. The battle had been won!

The injury Napoleon suffered bothered him for the rest of his life. But he thought it was a small price to pay for the glory he gained. After the victory, one official of the new government wrote to the minister of war that Napoleon had "plenty of knowledge, and as much intelligence and courage."

Napoleon certainly wasn't going to argue with that glowing praise. Because nobody thought more highly of Napoleon than Napoleon! "I promised you brilliant successes," he wrote to the minister of war. "As you see, I have kept my word." He was promoted from captain all the way to brigadier general, skipping several ranks in between.

CHAPTER 4
The Little Corporal

Napoleon helped defend the new government of France. But the new republican system was quickly replaced by an even newer one, called the Directory. And because the royalists were still putting up a fight, the Directory sent for Napoleon. They needed his experience and bravery.

On October 5, 1795, the royalists fought the republicans in Paris, outnumbering them six to one. But Napoleon wasn't worried. He had cleverly positioned dozens of cannons near the palace. He let the royalists almost reach the steps of the palace. When they were very close, he gave the order to fire. Immediately, hundreds of royalists fell dead in the streets.

It was a brutal attack. The Directory was saved, but many Frenchmen were killed. The royalists called it a brutal massacre. The Directory called it heroic. Napoleon was promoted to full general. Several months later, he was put in charge of the French army in Italy.

Napoleon's status as a hero made him a welcome guest in Paris society. He received invitations to many fashionable parties. But he was never very comfortable attending them. He was quiet and awkward around women. Then, in late October 1795, he met Rose de Beauharnais. She was the

widow of a royalist who had been executed during the French Revolution. Napoleon liked Rose, but he didn't like her name. He decided to call her Josephine instead!

Josephine was pretty, and she was charming. Napoleon was in love! He wanted to get married. Josephine liked Napoleon well enough, but she wasn't quite sure she loved him. But in the end, she married Napoleon. He was head over heels in love. "It is not in my power to have a single

thought which is not of thee," he wrote to her in one of many passionate letters.

Napoleon and Josephine were married on March 9, 1796. He was twenty-six years old. After the wedding, they spent only two days together before he went off to war. At the time, France was at war with several nations, including Austria and various Italian states.

Napoleon marched his men into Italy. The combined Austrian and Italian troops would have sixty-three thousand soldiers, if only they could meet up in time! Napoleon was trying to

prevent that from happening. His thirty-eight thousand men marched thirty miles a day to get to the Italian soldiers before the Austrians could catch up. His enemies marched only six or seven miles a day. The French defeated the Italians in the Piedmont region, then chased the Austrians to the city of Lodi, not far from Milan.

Italy 1794

During Napoleon's time, Italy was not a single country like it is today. It was made up of different kingdoms, republics, and duchies. (A duchy is a territory ruled by a duke or duchess.) Each region had its own government. Many included large cities that were centers for trading and business, such as Florence, Milan, Naples, Rome, and Venice.

It was not until 1861 that Italy became a unified country.

There, a single narrow bridge was all that stood between the French and victory. The Austrians defended the bridge. There was only one thing to do: charge! At great risk, Napoleon's men took the bridge and won the battle.

The men followed Napoleon's orders at Lodi even though the odds were against them. They knew that Napoleon was very aggressive, but he wasn't careless. He only entered a battle believing he would win. So his men believed it, too.

Before every battle, Napoleon gave an inspiring speech to fire up his troops. He also rewarded them with gold and valuables he took from his defeated enemies. For many years, French troops had earned very little pay. Now they were being rewarded with riches. They were also given awards and medals for their service. Napoleon would

personally go down the line of troops and praise or pat them on the shoulder. The soldiers felt as if he was one of them. And, in a way, he was.

Napoleon believed he could do any job in the military, and he sometimes did. That included everything from making guns and gunpowder to teaching strategy. At Lodi he aimed the cannons himself—a job usually done by a low-level soldier.

The men loved him for it. They called him *le petit caporal*, which means "the little corporal." (*Little* referred to the lowly rank of corporal.) Even though he was their general, Napoleon didn't hesitate to take on any of the small chores the other soldiers did.

Napoleon ate the same food as his men. His favorite meal before a battle was fried potatoes and onions. And on the battlefield, he wore an old gray overcoat instead of the colorful uniform of a general.

But while his men saw Napoleon as one of them, he thought of himself as above all other humans. The victory at Lodi convinced him of this. "From that moment, I foresaw what I might be," he later wrote. "Already I felt the earth flee from beneath me, as if I were being carried into the sky."

CHAPTER 5
Conquering Hero

In the story of his life, Napoleon imagined that he was as strong a leader as his hero, Alexander the Great. But how did other people see him? This was two hundred years before the Internet. He couldn't share his victories on Twitter. And he couldn't Instagram the moment of surrender by the opposing commander. Napoleon wanted very badly to present just the right image to the rest of the world.

So he began telling his story the way he wanted it told. He hired artists to paint pictures of his biggest accomplishments, including the victory at Lodi. He even wrote to the newspaper himself about how amazing the French army was.

Napoleon was ahead of his time in this area.

He was one of the first military leaders in history to see how important it was to have public opinion on his side. He even started his own newspapers because reports of some of his victories were not good enough! "Four hostile newspapers are more to be feared than a thousand bayonets," he said.

He took an active role in creating his brand. He instructed the artists exactly how he should appear in their paintings. He told them what the theme of the work should be. He was even specific about how big the frame should be. Sometimes he made sure the artist showed him fighting heroically in battle. Other times he wanted the artist to show him at rest or conducting business. In those paintings, Napoleon almost always has his hand inside his coat. That was to show how relaxed he was. He wanted to indicate to anyone who saw the painting that he was in charge.

And the public loved it! Napoleon's legend began to grow. He was only twenty-six years old when he marched his army into Milan in 1796. He was greeted as a hero who would free the people from the rule of their king. He became the political leader of Milan. In his story, he wasn't just a military hero who won battles but also a man who made life better for the people he conquered.

Napoleon knew he had a bigger and better army than many of his enemies. All healthy French men were required to join the military for at least five years. Many of them had grown up on farms and were used to carrying heavy loads in the hot sun. Making a thirty-mile march was no problem for them. By 1797, Napoleon had the best army in the world.

The British, though, had the best navy. "Wherever wood can swim, there I am sure to find this flag of England," Napoleon once said. He meant that the British navy was so good, its boats were "swimming" everywhere around the globe.

Napoleon wanted to control the trade routes that the British relied on to sail ships and cargo around the world. He had a plan to conquer Egypt and then build a canal linking the Red Sea to the Mediterranean Sea. The canal would create a more direct route for ships to sail from India

to western Europe. If the British traders couldn't
sail past Napoleon in Egypt along the coast of
the Mediterranean Sea, they wouldn't be able to
return to Great Britain.

Trade Routes

Much of the silk, spices, tea, and other goods used by the people of England in the late eighteenth century came from India. Sailing to England from India, though, required a lengthy voyage. Ships sailed from southeast Asia around the southern tip of Africa and then north to western Europe. The only other way to get from India to western Europe involved expensive and time-consuming land travel.

Napoleon did not succeed in building his canal before he returned to France. Eventually, an Egyptian corporation completed the Suez Canal, linking the Red Sea to the Mediterranean Sea, in 1869.

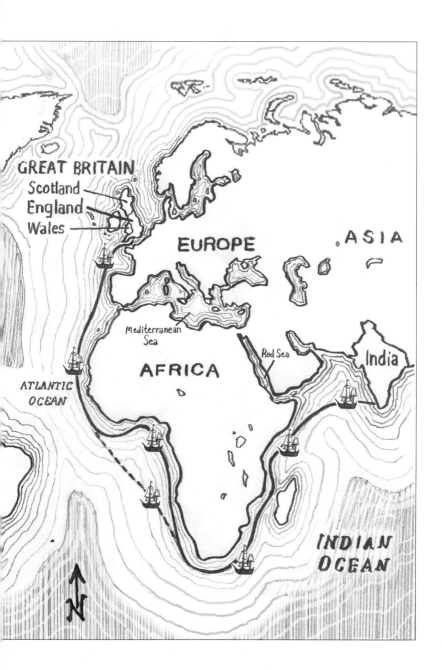

The plan to conquer Egypt started well. In 1798, Napoleon sailed from France with four hundred ships. He took not only forty thousand soldiers and ten thousand sailors, but also scientists, historians, and mathematicians to study Egyptian culture.

Napoleon had little trouble conquering the nation. The four million people who lived in Egypt at the time were led by competing tribes of warriors called Mamluks. The Mamluks used old-fashioned tactics and weapons to fight.

When the Mamluks charged at Napoleon's army on horseback carrying sabers (curved swords), the French army shot them with their guns. "The Battle of the Pyramids," as it was called, wasn't much of a battle. About thirty of Napoleon's men were killed, but as many as five to six thousand Mamluks died. Much of the Egyptian army was wiped out in about an hour.

Egyptian Mamluks

Napoleon marched into the capital city of Cairo and made himself ruler of Egypt. But then things took a turn for the worse. The British cornered Napoleon's ships in the Mediterranean Sea on August 1 and destroyed all but two. Napoleon's troops had no way to return to France! They were stranded in Egypt until they could rebuild their ships.

Napoleon decided to make the best of it. He began to study the culture he had conquered.

The experts he brought with him wrote a large book on Egyptian culture and history. They made many important discoveries, including the Rosetta Stone. Napoleon called his time in Egypt "the most beautiful of my life."

The Rosetta Stone

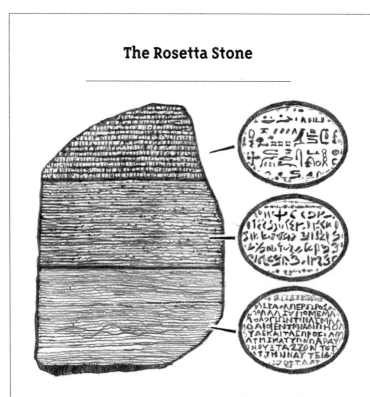

In July 1799, a French soldier discovered a large piece of stone with ancient writing on it near the city of Rosetta in Egypt. The stone had inscriptions in three different languages: an ancient Egyptian language called Demotic; hieroglyphs, another ancient Egyptian writing system that used pictures; and Greek.

What was written on the stone—which has become known as the Rosetta Stone—was not as important as the languages themselves.

For centuries, archaeologists had tried to understand hieroglyphs. Because they already knew Greek, the Rosetta Stone helped them translate the hieroglyphic pictures and symbols. Once the code was cracked, they began to understand ancient Egyptian traditions, culture, and history much better.

The Rosetta Stone was taken by British troops in 1801. It has been housed at the British Museum in London since 1802.

Back in France, the government was once again becoming unpopular. Prices were high. Food was scarce. Napoleon had heard the country was in trouble again. And on August 23, 1799, Napoleon abandoned his troops and sailed back to France on one of the two ships that survived the British attack a year earlier. The French people greeted him with great cheers. Who better to save the day than a man who had won battles all over Europe?

On November 10, 1799, Napoleon burst into a meeting of government officials in Paris called the Council of Five Hundred. Five hundred men had many different opinions about fixing France's problems. Some wanted a man like Napoleon to take charge. Some wanted to continue the government that had been in place since the end of the French Revolution. Some even wanted to go back to the monarchy.

"Outlaw!" screamed the officials who wanted

nothing to do with Napoleon. They tried to have him arrested. Napoleon's soldiers shielded him. His brother, Lucien, was a government official. He helped convince the Council of Five Hundred to put Napoleon in charge.

Lucien Bonaparte

No shots were fired, but Napoleon suddenly became the ruler of France!

He was one of three men in charge in a new government called the Consulate. But as first consul, Napoleon had the most power. He had successfully organized a coup d'état (say: COO day-TA)—an overthrow of the old government.

CHAPTER 6
Emperor

Napoleon quickly went to work. Over the next several years, he helped make big changes that made life better for the French people. He started government programs that built beautiful roads in Paris and bridges that crossed the River Seine. Other programs made banking easier and education better. And he helped create a set of laws called the Napoleonic Code.

Before Napoleon took over, the laws in France often depended more on a person's status and wealth than the ideas of right and wrong. The laws were also different from one town to another. It was all very confusing! Napoleon wanted to create a unified set of laws for the entire nation.

How did Napoleon get so much done? Well, he was always working! Even when he was at dinner or the theater, his mind was always on his work. Often he was going over papers or being briefed by an assistant. His meals were quick.

Unless he was at a fancy official dinner, he was usually done eating in ten minutes!

The Napoleonic Code

The Napoleonic Code established the basic right that all people are equal under the law. (Which, at the time, meant only that  all *men* were equal under the law.) The *Code Civil*, as it was called, ended the class system in France for good. It gave people the freedom to work at whatever jobs they chose and to practice their religions, or no religion at all. It also led to later laws that established rights for people who had been accused of crimes.

Because Napoleon brought his efficient code of administration and government to the nations he conquered, it influenced much of Europe. The Napoleonic Code remains the basic outline of the law in many parts of the world today.

At night, Napoleon would go to bed for a few hours, then wake up at three o'clock in the morning to start working again. His assistants said they rarely saw him tired, even after an eighteen-hour day.

When creating his *Code Civil*, for instance, Napoleon often worked until the early hours of the morning. He organized a commission to come up with a set of laws to be fair to everyone.

But he didn't let the group do all the work. He led many of the meetings himself.

Napoleon also had an amazing memory. He wasn't great with names and dates, but reportedly he could remember the exact position of two

cannons on a battlefield hundreds of miles from France!

Under Napoleon's leadership, the French economy improved. More people had steady jobs. Fewer people were starving. Napoleon's popularity grew and grew.

Napoleon used his power and his popularity to fill government positions with people who agreed with him. And in 1804, those people passed a law that made him emperor.

Napoleon, who had been married to Josephine for eight years, didn't have any children yet. But if he ever did, his title could be passed down from generation to generation. Of course, that sounds a lot like a monarchy—and the French Revolution was fought to end the rule of their king. But things were going well in France. So the French people didn't mind.

During this time, France seemed to constantly be at war. With every victory, Napoleon extended his empire farther into Europe. The French Empire grew to include many areas that are now part of Italy, Germany, Belgium, the Netherlands, and more.

In 1805, it looked as if Napoleon might try to add Great Britain to his list of conquests. He lined up troops along the French coastline, facing the English Channel. Britain had asked Russia and Austria to team up to defeat the French. But Napoleon had spies all over Europe. He knew what was happening. He turned his troops around and headed inland instead.

Napoleon quickly marched to Austria. There, on a field in the rural town of Austerlitz, he won his greatest victory. Even though his enemies had more men and more guns, he defeated the combined forces of Russia and Austria. It was a

bloody battle. Fifteen thousand of the enemy's ninety thousand troops were killed or injured, and nine thousand of France's sixty-eight thousand soldiers were killed.

At Austerlitz, Napoleon used one of his favorite strategies. On purpose, he left one part of his army exposed to an attack. Then, when the Austrian and Russian soldiers tried to move forward, he brought in the rest of his troops to swoop behind and surround them. By the time the enemy realized what was happening, it was too late.

At the time, most wars were fought with rows of soldiers arranged in lines straight across the battlefield. The lines would walk directly toward each other—and may the best men win! But one of Napoleon's favorite tactics was to split the enemy's line in two. He would have his soldiers drive straight through the center of his enemy's line. A smaller part of Napoleon's army would then hold off the one side, while the larger part of his army aggressively attacked the other side. After that attack was won, Napoleon's forces would join up to overwhelm the first side.

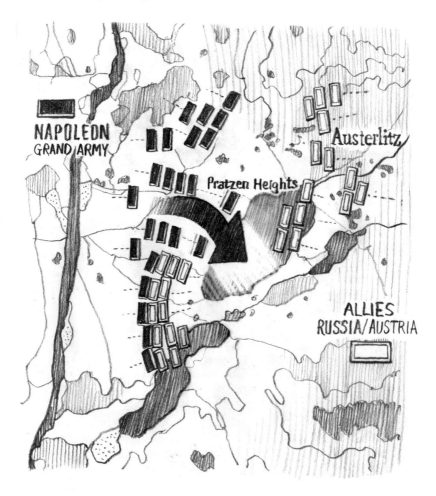

When news of the victory at Austerlitz reached France, the people there had a huge celebration. Before Austerlitz, Napoleon had already been considered a great military commander. After this battle, he was considered one of the best in the history of the world.

CHAPTER 7
Beginning of the End

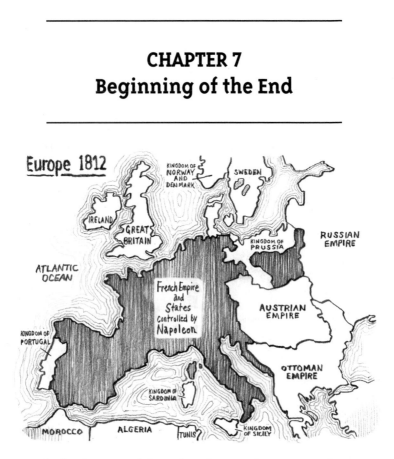

Europe 1812

At its largest, Napoleon's empire covered more than 800,000 square miles. It included parts of what is now Germany, Italy, the Netherlands, Poland, and Spain. In 1812, Napoleon ruled more than seventy million people.

Napoleon still wanted to add Great Britain to his list of conquests. But to get there, he had to cross the English Channel—and he knew he couldn't beat the British navy on the water. He was smart enough not to try.

Napoleon did not like the British, and the feeling was mutual. British newspaper cartoons were especially mean to Napoleon. They often made fun of him. In fact, that's why we now think of Napoleon as a very short man. The English newspapers always showed him as a tiny figure compared to the mighty British. At five feet seven inches, Napoleon was about the average height for his day. He just looked a lot smaller in the British drawings! And photography hadn't been invented yet to prove otherwise.

THE KING of BRODINGNAG and GULLIVER

Since he couldn't invade England, Napoleon decided to fight the British another way. He would try to hurt their economy. In 1806, Napoleon instituted the Continental System that made it illegal for any territory under French control to trade with Great Britain. British ships weren't even allowed into their ports. Many nations simply ignored the order so that they could continue to trade with the British. Other nations obeyed but lost a lot of money as they gave up trade opportunities.

The Continental System was a big mistake. But it was only the first of several that led to Napoleon's downfall.

At first the citizens of the countries that Napoleon had conquered were happy with his new ways of governing. But they quickly came to realize that Napoleon's rule was no better than the governments he had toppled. Napoleon needed his family to help control his empire, enforce his laws, and make the people pay very high taxes that funded his wars.

In 1808, Napoleon invaded Spain and made his brother Joseph the king. But the Spanish would not surrender. It was the start of a long and bloody war in Spain that was neither won nor lost.

King Joseph of Spain

Napoleon's brother Louis became king of Holland. Jerome was named king of Westphalia in northern Germany. Caroline, Elisa, and Pauline each ruled over different Italian states. Even Napoleon's mother received a fancy title: "Madam, the Mother of His Imperial Majesty The Emperor."

Madam, the Mother of His Imperial Majesty The Emperor

Unfortunately, it was his wife, Josephine, who seemed to no longer be useful to Napoleon.

Josephine was popular at home in France. "I win the wars, but she wins the people's hearts,"

Napoleon said. He still loved her. He didn't even mind too much that she spent one million francs a year—about $4 million in today's money!—on clothes. But he was very sad that they had no children. Napoleon desperately wanted a son who would one day be emperor. Josephine, who was in her midforties by 1809, could not have children. So Napoleon divorced her. She moved into one of their forty-four palaces. He gave her three million francs per year on which to live.

The next year, Napoleon married eighteen-year-old Marie-Louise of Austria.

Napoleon's second wife was the daughter of Francis II, the emperor of Austria. Because Austria was often at war with France, Marie-Louise grew up disliking Napoleon. But her father thought if they were married, it might help bring peace to the two countries.

Marie-Louise agreed to marry Napoleon to please her father. She traveled to Paris and met Napoleon for the first time just five days before the wedding on April 1, 1810. "You are much better looking than your portrait," she told him.

In 1811, Napoleon and Marie-Louise had a son. The baby was given the name Napoleon François Joseph Charles Bonaparte and the title "king of Rome." By all accounts, Napoleon was a good father when he was with his son. But he wasn't cut out to be a stay-at-home dad. At heart, he was a soldier who was most at home on the battlefield.

Napoleon II: the king of Rome

So Napoleon stayed ready for war. And in 1812, after the Russians broke the deal they had agreed to under the Continental System, he made the worst error of his career: He invaded Russia.

In the summer of that year, Napoleon marched to Russia with six hundred thousand men.

The invasion was a disaster. Napoleon expected the Russian army to meet him near the border, be amazed at his own massive army, and surrender. He didn't count on the Russians retreating to the interior of their huge country. But, as winter came,

Napoleon followed the Russian army farther and farther from home.

After winning the Battle of Borodino, he entered Moscow, Russia's largest and most famous city. He found the Russians had burned their own city to the ground. There was no food.

Winter came, and Napoleon had to retreat. By the time he arrived in France, over five hundred thousand of his men had either been killed in battle, starved to death, fell to disease, or had simply given up and left the army. Only ninety-three thousand soldiers returned with him.

Napoleon's failure in Russia encouraged several nations, including Austria, Great Britain, and Spain, to band together and march to France to fight against him.

The French people had been at war since 1792. Almost always, though, the battles had been fought somewhere else. By late 1813, the war had arrived in their country. They were not happy about it. Public opinion started to turn against the emperor.

Napoleon could have signed a peace treaty with his enemies. The French borders would have returned to about where they had been before he started his empire expansion. France could have finally been at peace. And Napoleon might have remained in charge. But that was not enough for him. Napoleon was too proud, and he refused the terms.

The French army fell to the coalition—the group of countries that Napoleon had fought so hard to control—in April 1814. Napoleon was forced to step down from his role as emperor. He was forty-four years old. Louis XVIII, the younger brother of the former king of France,

Louis XVIII

became king. The coalition banished Napoleon
from France.

CHAPTER 8
Exile

Napoleon sailed to the tiny island of Elba, six miles off the coast of Italy, on April 28, 1814. He was given the title "emperor of Elba" as a cruel joke. But Napoleon was as ambitious as

ever. Before he arrived, he had designed a flag for Elba. Once there, he made plans for organizing an army and a navy, setting up a court system, and paving roads.

About twelve thousand people lived on Elba, including Napoleon's large staff and one thousand or so French soldiers that arrived with him. He lived in a big house with several servants. His second wife, Marie-Louise, and their son had fled to her father's home in Austria. Napoleon never saw them again. Nor did he see Josephine. But his mother, Letizia, came to live with him. His sister Pauline helped arrange his schedule. Napoleon gave many parties and had many visitors.

And yet, he was bored. He waited for a chance to get off the island. After ten months, it came. On February 26, 1815, he and six hundred of his soldiers sailed from Elba. They arrived in France three days later and began marching to Paris.

King Louis XVIII discovered that Napoleon was back in France, and he sent his army to stop him. When the soldiers came close, Napoleon walked toward them alone. He invited any of the men to shoot him if they wanted. But he knew the king's soldiers still admired him. They shouted, "Long live the emperor!" and escorted him to Paris.

The king fled the city. As soon as the coalition of nations found out that Napoleon was back in Paris, it sent forces to defeat him. It didn't take long. Napoleon put up a fight, winning several battles. But on June 18, 1815, he was defeated at the Battle of Waterloo (in what is now Belgium).

Four days later, he gave up his rule again. This time it was for good. Napoleon had regained control of France for 111 days, now known as the "Hundred Days."

And this time, the coalition didn't take any chances. Napoleon was sent to an even smaller island, with a smaller house and a smaller staff. He was guarded by coalition soldiers twenty-four hours a day.

The island was Saint Helena, in the middle of the Atlantic Ocean. It was controlled by the British and covered only forty-seven square miles. Two British naval ships patrolled the island around the clock. There would be no escaping this time. Napoleon had little to do on Saint Helena. He read and he gardened. He dictated his life story to his assistants. He was sure, of course, to tell it in a way that made him look good.

After living on the island for five years, Napoleon became sick. He grew weaker and

weaker. On May 5, 1821, he died at age fifty-one. There was a rumor at the time that he had been poisoned. More likely, he died from stomach cancer, the same disease that had killed his father.

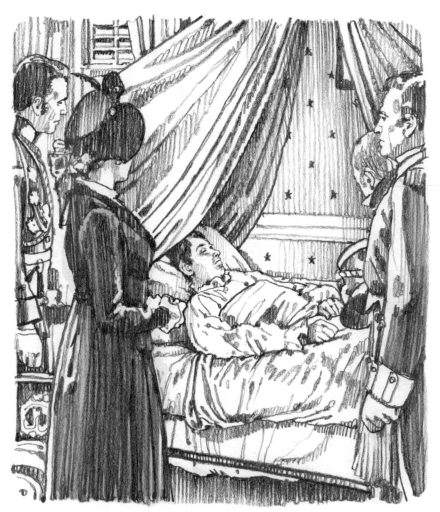

At first, Napoleon was buried on Saint Helena. Then, in 1840, the British agreed to move his body back to Paris. Napoleon's body now rests in

the Dome des Invalides, a large church that is the burial site of some of France's most famous war heroes. It is a popular spot for tourists.

More than two centuries after his death, many details of Napoleon's life are still fascinating to us. In Corsica, Napoleon's boyhood home is a national museum. The island holds an annual festival each year to remember his birthday. In France, Napoleon is a national hero whose conquests brought power and glory to the nation. Under his rule, lasting changes such as the Napoleonic Code, the bank of France, and freedom of religion were established.

Not everyone agrees that Napoleon should be considered a hero. He had many enemies, and many people died in wars that he started. Almost everyone does agree, however, that Napoleon was one of the greatest military commanders ever—and maybe *the* greatest of all time.

Timeline of Napoleon's Life

1769 — Napoleon Bonaparte is born on the island of Corsica on August 15

1779 — Begins military school in France

1785 — Becomes an artillery lieutenant in the French army

1793 — Defeats royalists at Toulon and is promoted to brigadier general

1795 — Defends the revolutionary government from rebels in Paris

1796 — Marries Josephine de Beauharnais

1797 — Defeats the Austrian army in Italy

1798 — Invades Egypt

1799 — As first consul, becomes the leader of the French government

1804 — Becomes emperor of France

— Institutes the Napoleonic Code

1809 — Divorces Josephine

1810 — Marries Marie-Louise of Austria

1811 — Son, Napoleon II, is born

1812 — Invades Russia

1814 — Gives up the throne for the first time and is exiled to Elba

1815 — Escapes from Elba and returns to the throne

— Loses Battle of Waterloo and is exiled to Saint Helena

1821 — Dies on Saint Helena on May 5

Timeline of the World

1775 — Start of the American Revolutionary War

1776 — The Declaration of Independence establishes the United States of America as a new nation

1783 — Twelve-year-old German composer Ludwig van Beethoven publishes his first works

1789 — Start of the French Revolution in Paris

1793 — American Eli Whitney invents the cotton gin

1796 — The first successful vaccine, for smallpox, is introduced

1800 — Italy's Alessandro Volta introduces an electric battery

1801 — The United Kingdom of Great Britain and Ireland is established

1803 — The United States doubles in size with the Louisiana Purchase from France

1804 — Captain Meriwether Lewis and Second Lieutenant William Clark begin their famous expedition to explore what is now the western United States

1807 — The first commercial steamboat sails in the United States

1809 — Abraham Lincoln is born in Hodgenville, Kentucky, on February 12

1812 — Great Britain and the United States wage the War of 1812

1814 — The first practical steam locomotive is built

Bibliography

*Books for young readers

*Burleigh, Robert. ***Napoleon: The Story of the Little Corporal***.
New York: Abrams Books for Young Readers, 2007.

*Carroll, Bob. ***Napoleon Bonaparte***. San Diego, CA: Lucent Books,
1994.

*Greenblatt, Miriam. ***Napoleon Bonaparte and Imperial France***.
Tarrytown, NY: Marshall Cavendish Benchmark, 2006.

*Heuston, Kimberley. ***Napoleon: Emperor and Conqueror***.
New York: Franklin Watts, 2010.

Johnson, Paul. ***Napoleon: A Life***. New York: Penguin Group, 2002.

*Landau, Elaine. ***Napoleon Bonaparte***. Minneapolis, MN:
Twenty-First Century Books, 2006.

Roberts, Andrew. ***Napoleon: A Life***. New York: Viking, 2014.